D0912905

Stories of *Titanic's*

THIRD CLASS

BY PEGGY CARAVANTES

Published by The Child's World®
1980 Lookout Drive • Mankato, MN 56003-1705
800-599-READ • www.childsworld.com

Acknowledgments
The Child's World®: Mary Berendes, Publishing Director
Red Line Editorial: Design, editorial direction, and production
Photographs ©: George Grantham Bain Collection/Library of Congress, cover, 1, 4; Chitose Suzuki/AP Images, 6; AP Images, 8; William H. Pierce/Library of Congress, 10; Bettmann/Corbis, 12, 19; Matthew Polak/Sygma/Corbis, 15; Underwood & Underwood/Corbis, 16, 20

ISBN 9781634074681

LCCN 2015946339

Printed in the United States of America
Mankato, MN
December, 2015
PA02287

ABOUT THE AUTHOR

After a career in education, Peggy Caravantes fulfilled a lifetime dream to write. She is the author of numerous children's history books and middle-grade and young-adult biographies. Caravantes holds a bachelor of arts degree with a major in English and a master of educational administration degree. She lives in San Antonio, Texas.

Table of CONTENTS

Chapter 1

DISASTER ON THE *TITANIC*

On the evening of Sunday, April 14, 1912, the *Titanic* cruised across the Atlantic Ocean. It was the fifth day of the grand ship's first voyage from England to America. Laura Cribb, a 16-year-old passenger in third class, looked at the sky. "The weather was fine and the stars were bright,"

◀ The *Titanic* was the largest ship of its time.

she later remembered.[1] Laura and her father, John, stayed up late, talking and looking at the ocean.

The *Titanic* had already completed more than half of its trip. On board were 2,223 people. More than 700 passengers, including the Cribbs, had bought the cheapest tickets, in third class. Most third-class passengers were European **emigrants**. They were looking for a better life in the United States. Though the *Titanic* set off from England, these passengers came from many different countries.

Third-class passengers were housed in the lowest part of the ship, called steerage. Their rooms were simple compared to the more expensive first-class spaces. There were 84 third-class **cabins**. Most had beds for four to six people. The third-class passengers slept in crowded conditions. But they enjoyed fresh water, heat, and electricity. These were not found in third-class rooms on many other ships.

While Laura Cribb was looking at the stars, other third-class travelers had a party. Annie Kelly, a 20-year-old, attended the party with people from her county in Ireland. The group hoped to find homes and work in Chicago, Illinois. Annie enjoyed gatherings and had already made new friends on board.

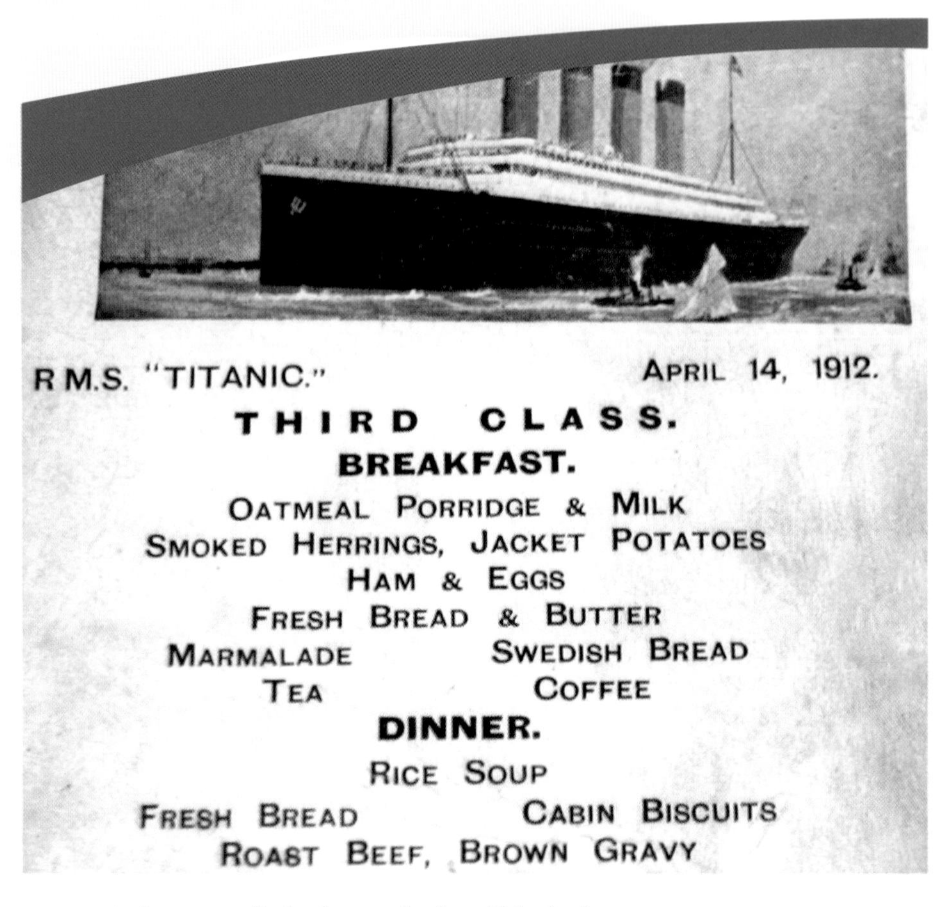

R M.S. "TITANIC." APRIL 14, 1912.

THIRD CLASS.

BREAKFAST.

OATMEAL PORRIDGE & MILK

SMOKED HERRINGS, JACKET POTATOES

HAM & EGGS

FRESH BREAD & BUTTER

MARMALADE SWEDISH BREAD

TEA COFFEE

DINNER.

RICE SOUP

FRESH BREAD CABIN BISCUITS

ROAST BEEF, BROWN GRAVY

▲ A menu listed meals for third-class passengers on the *Titanic*.

At 10:00 p.m., the ship's **stewards** turned out the lights, ending the good times. Annie and her friends went to their cabins to sleep. But at 11:40 p.m., they were jolted awake by a massive **collision**. Passengers didn't know it yet, but the *Titanic* had crashed into a giant iceberg.

At first, stewards told the passengers not to worry. But the iceberg had created large holes in the ship. It began to flood with water. By midnight, crew members rushed through the halls and knocked on doors. "All hands on deck!" they shouted. "Hurry if you would have a chance for your lives!"[2]

The crew helped people into lifeboats. But third-class passengers had to wait until first- and second-class travelers were loaded into the boats. Only a small number of third-class passengers were given spaces.

Laura Cribb was one of the lucky ones. During the voyage, John Cribb befriended some sailors. They had taken him to parts of the ship not usually shown to third-class passengers. When John felt the jar of the collision, he led Laura through a crew-only passage. There, he helped Laura into Lifeboat #12. Laura's lifeboat had a full load of about 70 passengers. They rowed the boat out to sea.

Annie Kelly was also lucky. When the crash happened, she and her roommates ran into the hall in their nightgowns. Her friend, a steward, led her upstairs. On deck, he saw a boat that was about to be lowered into the water. He pushed Annie into the boat and yelled, "Let this young girl go with you. You've got room. Let her in."[3] She became the final passenger in Lifeboat #16, the last regular lifeboat **launched**. Hundreds of third-class passengers remained on the sinking ship. They still needed rescue.

Chapter 2

SAVED BY A COLLAPSIBLE BOAT

After the lifeboats left, water continued to fill the *Titanic*. The damaged side of the ship was leaning into the water. The upper deck was slanting so much that it was only about 5 feet (1.5 m) above the water. The only way to survive was to get into a **collapsible** boat. There were just four of these boats on the ship. Each could hold

◀ **After it hit an iceberg, the *Titanic* began to sink.**

up to 47 people. Crew members helped people into Collapsible Boat A.

Rhoda Abbott and her two teenage sons, Rossmoor and Eugene, waited to get in the boat. They were traveling back to Providence, Rhode Island. The family had been living with Rhoda's mother in England.

As the Abbotts waited, a huge wave of water washed across the ship. Collapsible Boat A fell into the ocean. Its **canvas** sides had not been raised high enough to keep out the water. The people now in the boat had to stand in water up to their knees. Several lost their balance and fell out.

Rhoda knew she had to act quickly to survive. She grabbed her sons' hands. Together, they jumped into the dark water. They swam to Collapsible Boat A. Rhoda and the boys clung to the sides of the boat. But the boys' hands began to slip. Waves swept them away from Rhoda. She shouted their names over and over, but it was no use. Her sons were gone, lost in the darkness. Eventually, someone pulled Rhoda into the boat. She stood with the other passengers in thigh-deep icy water.

Another passenger in Collapsible Boat A was 25-year-old Olaus Abelseth from Norway. He was returning to South Dakota

▲ **Icebergs can be very dangerous to ships.**

after a visit home. Olaus was traveling with his brother-in-law and a cousin. They were asleep when the *Titanic* hit the iceberg. Hearing the crash, Olaus dressed and went to find out what had happened. He noticed blocks of ice on the floors in the hallways.

Although a steward said there was no danger, Olaus did not believe him. Olaus went back to wake his relatives.

For a long time, Olaus and his family were not allowed to leave steerage. Finally, at about 2:00 a.m., a steward let them go upstairs. There were no boats left. Olaus knew they would have to jump. But neither of his relatives could swim. Olaus would have to help them.

Olaus clasped his brother-in-law's hand and jumped into the water. His cousin jumped at the same time. Olaus got tangled in some ropes. He had to let go of his brother-in-law's hand to free himself. Soon, waves swept away both of his relatives. Olaus said to himself, "I'm a goner."[4] All around him were men who knew they would not survive. But Olaus broke free of the ropes and began to swim.

In the distance, Olaus saw a dark object and headed in that direction. It was Collapsible Boat A. He began to climb in. People already on board warned him, "Don't **capsize** the boat."[5] But Olaus got in safely. He moved his arms constantly to stay warm. Olaus later explained, "We did not talk very much, except that we would say, 'One, two, three,' and scream together for help."[6]

Chapter 3

DANGEROUS WATERS

While sailors struggled to launch the other collapsible boats, steerage passengers realized the danger they faced. A 21-year-old man named Daniel Buckley had been traveling to the United States to start a new life. On the night of the crash, he was sleeping in a small third-class cabin. Daniel woke when he heard the terrible collision. When he jumped out of his **berth**, he stepped into water.

◀ **An artist illustrated the sinking of the *Titanic*.**

Daniel dressed and went outside the cabin to see what was happening. Two sailors ran down the halls. They were shouting, "All up on deck unless you want to get drowned!"[7]

Daniel hurried up the stairs to the Boat Deck. Everyone else on the deck had a lifebelt. Daniel had forgotten his and started back downstairs to get it. But the stairs he had just used were flooded. Luckily, a first-class passenger gave an extra lifebelt to Daniel.

When Daniel reached the upper decks, he ran into a locked gate. Another third-class passenger was kicking at the gate. A guard shoved the man down the steps. The furious passenger picked himself up. He charged at the gate, kicking it open. Third-class passengers rushed upward. On the upper deck, Daniel noticed a group of men trying to get into Collapsible Boat C. He joined the crowd, but officers ordered all the men out. They warned that only women and children were allowed into the lifeboats.

By then, Daniel was crying with fear. He snuck in the bottom of the boat. A kind woman placed a shawl over Daniel's head. She told him to be still. The officer could not see Daniel. The boat shoved off.

Another young man, Eugene Daly, was traveling to the United States with his cousin and a neighbor, both girls. When the *Titanic* hit the iceberg, the impact almost threw him out of his berth. Eugene woke and dressed quickly. A steward told Eugene that the collision was not serious. He advised the young man to go back to bed.

Instead, Eugene woke the two girls. They went to get lifebelts. The three managed to get to the second-class deck. There, the girls got into Lifeboat #15. Eugene tried to join them, but officers pulled him out. He went up to the first-class deck. Many people crowded around, waiting for a lifeboat. Eugene was too late. By the time he reached the front of the crowd, the lifeboats had all launched.

Water rushed over the deck as the *Titanic* sank lower into the ocean. Eugene jumped overboard. He found Collapsible Boat B a short distance from the sinking ship. It was flipped over, but Eugene and five other men climbed on top. The men helped passengers nearby get on the boat. Freezing water pooled around their legs, and a few passengers died on the boat. Then, three hours after the first lifeboat left the *Titanic*, the survivors spotted a ship in the distance.

Only some of the third-class passengers were rescued ▶ by lifeboats.

Chapter 4

SAFE AT LAST

Passengers in the lifeboats and collapsible boats faced a cold night at sea. The boats drifted for hours before the passengers were rescued. People used matches to light papers and cloths on fire. They held up these torches in the hope that someone on a larger ship would see the flames. Finally, at 4:00 a.m., a sailor aboard the RMS *Carpathia* spotted the lifeboats.

◀ **Crowds in New York rushed to greet *Titanic* survivors on the *Carpathia*.**

The ship neared the survivors. Sailors used ropes and burlap bags to haul them onto the ship. By 8:30 a.m., all the survivors were on board. Crew members gave them blankets, food, and water. The *Carpathia* headed for New York.

Officers on the *Carpathia* treated third-class passengers differently than the other survivors. After Laura Cribb was rescued, the officers asked her which class ticket she had on the *Titanic*. Survivors were given different food and areas to stay based on their class. The third-class section on the *Carpathia* was crowded and uncomfortable. It was much worse than the steerage area on the *Titanic*.

Though the survivors had been rescued, their nightmare was not yet over. Many had lost loved ones. Years after her rescue, Laura recalled her father: "I did not see him again. But, oh, the awfulness of it all did not come to me until long afterward."[8]

Many survivors needed treatment for medical problems. Annie Kelly was almost frozen when the *Carpathia* rescued her. She had been wearing only her nightgown all night. Sailors brought Annie hot drinks and warm blankets. But she could barely speak. When the *Carpathia* landed in New York, doctors rushed Annie to St. Vincent's Hospital. When she left the hospital six weeks later, she still wore her nightgown and a coat and shoes donated to her. Unable to forget all who died, Annie devoted her life to helping others.

After she lost both of her teenage sons, Rhoda Abbott faced months of hospital treatment. By the time the *Carpathia* got to New York, her legs were so frost-bitten they looked burned. Rhoda stayed in the hospital for two months. In the years afterward, she often talked about her sons. "I have [Eugene's] sled now that he used to enjoy," she wrote to a friend. "I miss him so much."[9]

Like Rhoda, Olaus Abelseth sat for over an hour in the freezing water. As Olaus was brought on board the *Carpathia*, he received a warm blanket and coffee. But with limited space on the ship, Olaus slept on the floor in his soaking-wet clothes.

Later, the United States Senate held hearings on the *Titanic* disaster. Senators wanted to find out how to prevent similar disasters. Olaus was one of only three third-class passengers called to **testify**. He described the horror of the *Titanic* collision and the bravery of the survivors.

Daniel Buckley was another third-class passenger who answered the Senate's questions. He spoke about how thankful he was for his rescue. But people learned that Daniel had hidden in the rescue boat under a woman's shawl. Some called him a coward. Others wanted to help him rebuild his life. The American Red Cross gave Daniel $100 for clothing and a place to stay.

Eugene Daly was also rescued by the *Carpathia* crew. Eugene could not forget the screams of the people who did not get

▲ **On the *Carpathia*, Captain Arthur Rostron and the crew helped survivors from the *Titanic*.**

▲ On the *Carpathia*, survivors from the *Titanic* bundled up in warm blankets.

into a boat. He had lost everything, including his money and his treasured bagpipes, on the *Titanic*. He struggled to afford food and housing in New York. Eventually, the company that owned the *Titanic* paid Eugene for his lost property. He bought a new set of bagpipes and found work as a musician.

On the night the *Titanic* sank, crew members cried, "Women and children first!" Yet fewer than half of the women and children in steerage were rescued. By comparison, almost all women and children in first class were rescued. Very few third-class men survived. A total of 462 men had traveled in steerage. Of these men, 387 died at sea.

There were several reasons that few third-class passengers survived. One reason was their location. They were housed in the bottom of the ship, far from the decks where lifeboats were launched. Even when the passengers reached the lifeboats, they were not allowed to board right away. In many cases, first-class and second-class passengers boarded before them. Also, many steerage passengers did not speak English. Some could not understand instructions from the crew. Getting from steerage to the Boat Deck required going through unfamiliar stairs and halls. Most third-class passengers did not arrive on the deck in time to get into one of the 20 lifeboats. Some lifeboats were not full when they launched. But even if they had been, there were not enough lifeboats for all of the passengers.

The U.S. Senate hearings about the *Titanic* led to more safety laws for ships. Other countries and organizations also adopted new safety rules. One new rule was that ships had to carry enough lifeboats for all passengers. While this rule was too late to help people on the *Titanic*, it helped protect passengers on other ships.

GLOSSARY

berth (BURTH): A berth is a place to sleep on a ship or train. A passenger ran out of her berth when she heard the crash.

cabins (KA-binz): Cabins are rooms where passengers stay and sleep on a ship. Families on the *Titanic* stayed in cabins.

canvas (KAN-vuhs): Canvas is a heavy, coarse cloth often used for tents and sails. On the *Titanic*, the collapsible boats were made of canvas.

capsize (KAP-seyes): To capsize a boat is to cause it to turn over. Passengers tried not to capsize the lifeboats.

collapsible (kuh-LAP-suh-bul): When something is collapsible, it can be folded. The *Titanic* crew helped passengers into collapsible boats.

collision (kuh-LI-zhuhn): A collision is a bump or a crash. A collision with an iceberg caused the *Titanic* to sink.

emigrants (EM-ih-grunts): Emigrants are people who leave a nation to settle in another country. Many *Titanic* passengers were emigrants from Europe.

launched (LONCHED): When a boat is launched, it is moved into the water. The crew on the *Titanic* launched the lifeboats.

stewards (STOO-erds): Stewards are helpers who take care of the passengers on ships. The stewards showed the passengers to their cabins.

testify (TESS-ti-fy): When people testify, they give evidence. Some *Titanic* survivors were asked to testify about the disaster.

SOURCE NOTES

1. "Laura's Account of the Night She Lost Her Papa." *Daily Echo*. Gannett, 9 April 2012. Web. 20 May 2015.

2. Senan Molony. *The Irish aboard Titanic*. Dublin: Wolfhound, 2000. Print. 100–101.

3. Ibid.

4. Walter Lord. *A Night to Remember.* New York: Henry Holt, 1955. Print. 99.

5. Hannah Holman. *Titanic Voices*. Gloucestershire, UK: Amberley, 2011. Print. 406.

6. Ibid.

7. Richard Davenport-Hines. *Voyagers of the Titanic.* New York: William Morrow, 2012. Print. 218.

8. Hannah Holman. *Titanic Voices*. Gloucestershire, UK: Amberley, 2011. Print. 153.

9. Hugh Brewster. *Gilded Lives, Fatal Voyage*. New York: Crown, 2012. Print. 273.

TO LEARN MORE

Books

Brown, Don. *All Stations! Distress! April 15, 1912, The Day the Titanic Sank*. New York: Square Fish, 2010.

Donnelly, Judy. *The Titanic Lost . . . and Found*. New York: Random House, 2010.

The Story of the Titanic. New York: DK Publishing, 2012.

Web Sites

Visit our Web site for links about the *Titanic*'s third class:
childsworld.com/links

Note to Parents, Teachers, and Librarians: We routinely verify our Web links to make sure they are safe and active sites. So encourage your readers to check them out!

INDEX